The Coming of the Pakeha

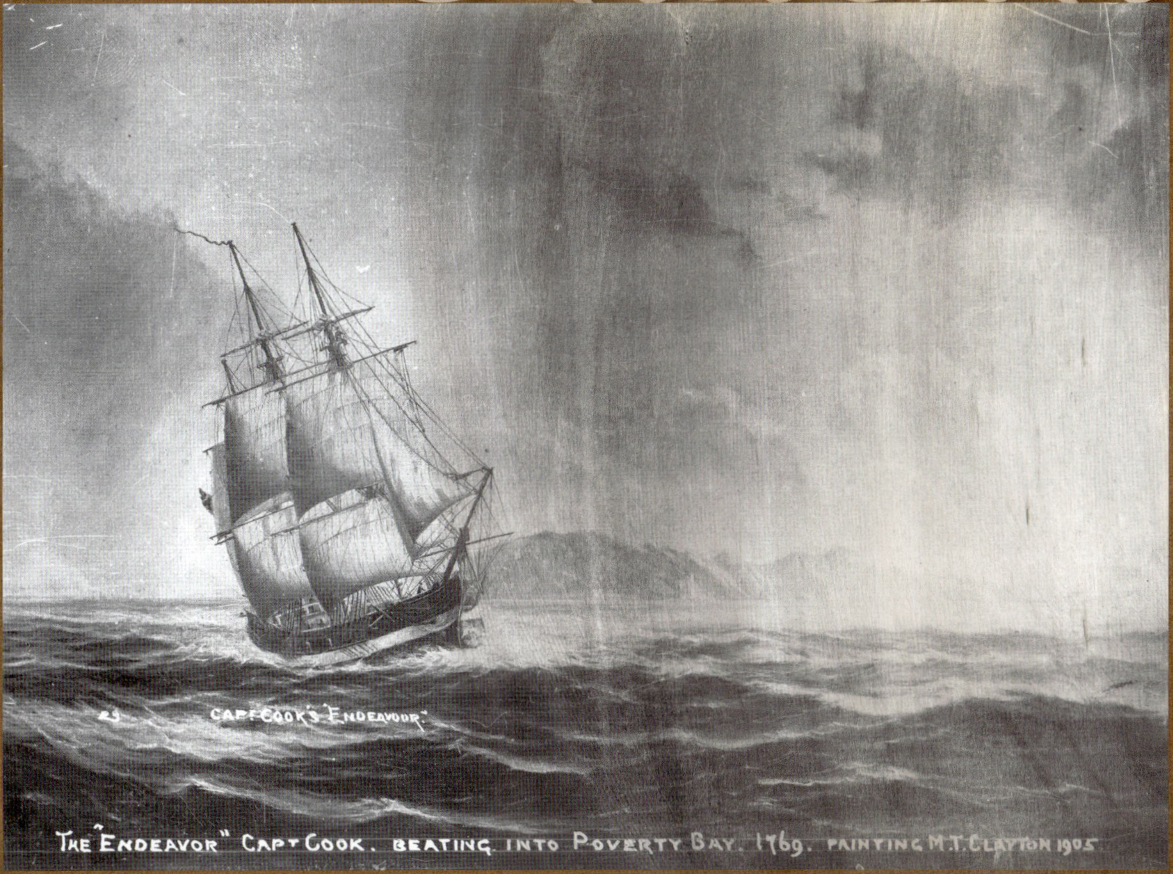

The "Endeavor" Capt Cook. Beating into Poverty Bay. 1769. Painting M.T. Clayton 1905

Capt Cook's Endeavour

John Lockyer

A RAUPO BOOK
Published by the Penguin Group
Penguin Group (NZ), 67 Apollo Drive, Rosedale,
North Shore 0632, New Zealand (a division of Pearson New Zealand Ltd)
Penguin Group (USA) Inc., 375 Hudson Street,
New York, New York 10014, USA
Penguin Group (Canada), 90 Eglinton Avenue East, Suite 700, Toronto,
Ontario, M4P 2Y3, Canada (a division of Pearson Penguin Canada Inc.)
Penguin Books Ltd, 80 Strand, London, WC2R 0RL, England
Penguin Ireland, 25 St Stephen's Green,
Dublin 2, Ireland (a division of Penguin Books Ltd)
Penguin Group (Australia), 250 Camberwell Road, Camberwell,
Victoria 3124, Australia (a division of Pearson Australia Group Pty Ltd)
Penguin Books India Pvt Ltd, 11, Community Centre,
Panchsheel Park, New Delhi – 110 017, India
Penguin Books (South Africa) (Pty) Ltd, 24 Sturdee Avenue,
Rosebank, Johannesburg 2196, South Africa

Penguin Books Ltd, Registered Offices: 80 Strand, London, WC2R 0RL, England

First published by Penguin Group (NZ), 2008
1 3 5 7 9 10 8 6 4 2

Copyright © John Lockyer 2008

The right of John Lockyer to be identified as the author of this work in terms of
section 96 of the Copyright Act 1994 is hereby asserted.

Designed by Cheryl Rowe
Printed in China

ISBN 978 1 86978 059 3

A catalogue record for this book is available
from the National Library of New Zealand.

www.penguin.co.nz

Contents

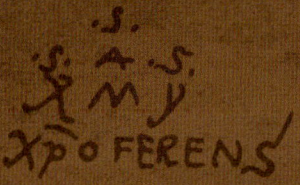
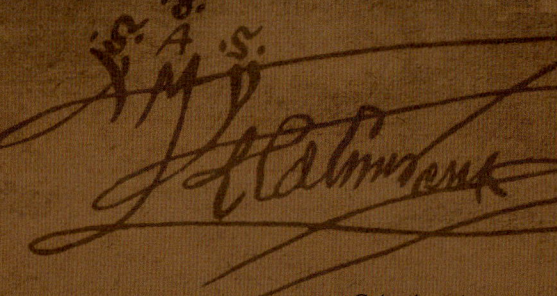

Seventeenth-century European Explorers

Explorers from Europe had much-improved ships and navigation methods during the early 1600s, and they were exploring the oceans of the unknown world. Christopher Columbus had discovered America and Francis Drake had sailed around the world.

Other explorers were searching for a large continent in the South Seas, the 'Southern Continent'. Mapmakers believed the continent would be rich in gold, silver and spices. They also believed that the large continent in the south balanced the land masses in the north.

At the same time, in New Zealand, Maori did not know there were people in the world who looked, thought and behaved differently than themselves.

Drake map

Abel Tasman

In 1642, Commander Abel Janszoon Tasman left Batavia (now Jakarta) with two ships, the *Zeehaen* and the *Heemskirk*, to find the southern continent. Batavia was a port on the island of Java in the Dutch East Indies (now Indonesia). On 13 December 1642, after sailing for 121 days, Tasman saw mountains. He wrote, 'towards noon, we saw a large land, uplifted high …'

*T*asman called the new land 'Staeten Landt'.

'*S*taeten Landt' was later renamed Zealandia Nova by Dutch mapmakers.

At the time of Tasman's discovery, the western coast of Australia was called Hollandia Nova. Holland and Zeeland are neighbouring sea provinces in the Netherlands.

Abel Tasman's discovery ships, the Zeehaen *and the* Heemskirk.
Alexander Turnbull Library, Wellington, New Zealand, PAColl-3053-01

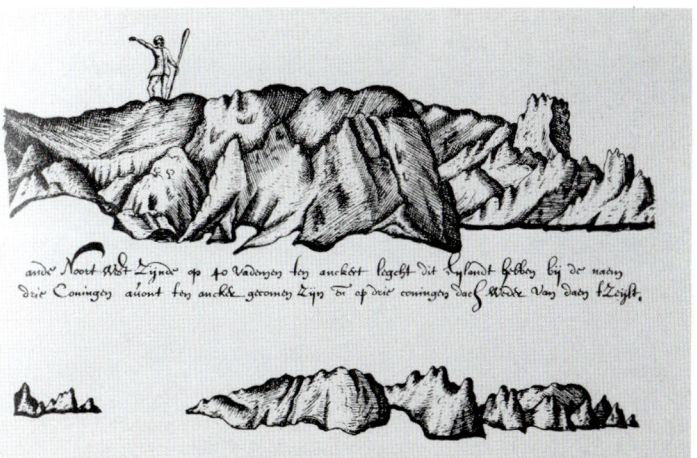

Isaac Gilsemans sketched the Three Kings Islands when Tasman's ships anchored there 'on [the] *Twelfth Night Eve …'*
Isaac Gilsemans, Alexander Turnbull Library, Wellington, New Zealand, PUBL-0086-019

Tasman sailed up the coast and around Farewell Spit. His ships anchored in a large bay. Maori paddled out from the shore in two double-hulled canoes. They called out and blew a trumpet-like instrument to challenge the visitors. The sailors called back and blew their own trumpets, unknowingly accepting a challenge. A short while later a boat being rowed between Tasman's ships was rammed by a canoe, which resulted in four sailors being killed.

Tasman had orders not to fight. He named the place Murderers' Bay, then began to sail up the North Island coast. Not able to find a safe place to land and without stepping ashore, Tasman left 'Staeten Landt' behind on 6 January 1643.

More than a century passed before Europeans returned.

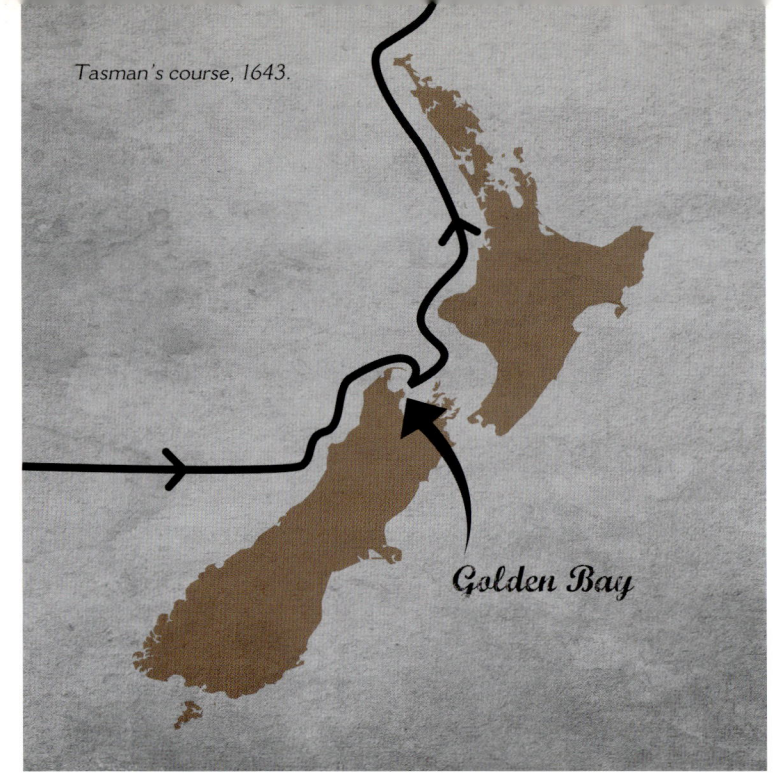

Tasman's course, 1643.

Golden Bay

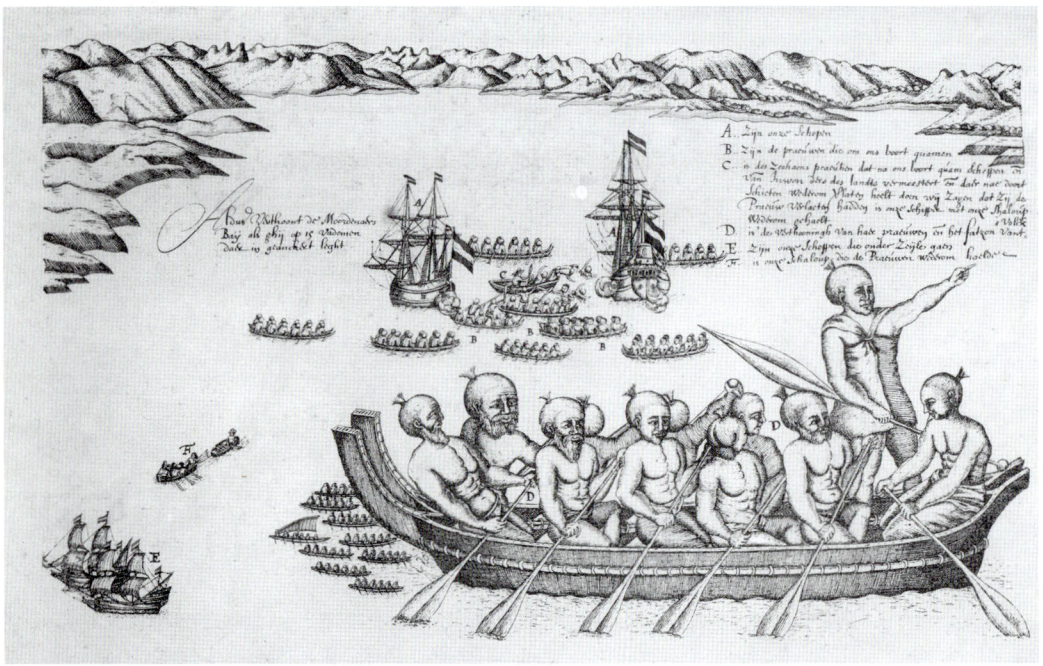

Gilsemans' text translates as, '**A** our ships **B** the prows which came alongside of us **C** the cock-boat of the Zeehan [sic], which came paddling towards our ship and was overpowered by the natives, who afterwards left it again owing to our firing, when we saw that they had left the cock-boat, our skipper fetched it back **D** a view of the native prow with the appearance of the people **E** our ships pulling off to sea **F** our pinnace bring back the cock-boat.' The *Heemskerck is at left.*

Isaac Gilsemans, Alexander Turnbull Library, Wellington, New Zealand, PUBL-0086-021

6

In 1769, James Cook renamed Murderers Bay. He called it Golden Bay.

Tasman and New Zealand placenames

Cape Maria Van Dieman and Three Kings Islands were named by Abel Tasman. There are several places named after Tasman, the most obvious being the Tasman Sea and Tasmania (Australia). In the South Island of New Zealand, there is the Abel Tasman National Park.

James Cook

In July 1769, Lieutenant James Cook of the British Royal Navy left Tahiti in the *Endeavour* and sailed south to the land discovered by Tasman, at that point called New Zealand. Cook made three voyages and four visits to New Zealand. He spent 328 days on and around the coast of the country.

On the *Endeavour*, Cook took Joseph Banks, a passenger with an interest in botany. Banks collected and catalogued new plants, birds and insects. Cook also had an artist on

Captain James Cook (1728–79).
John Webber, Alexander Turnbull Library, Wellington, New Zealand, C-051-015

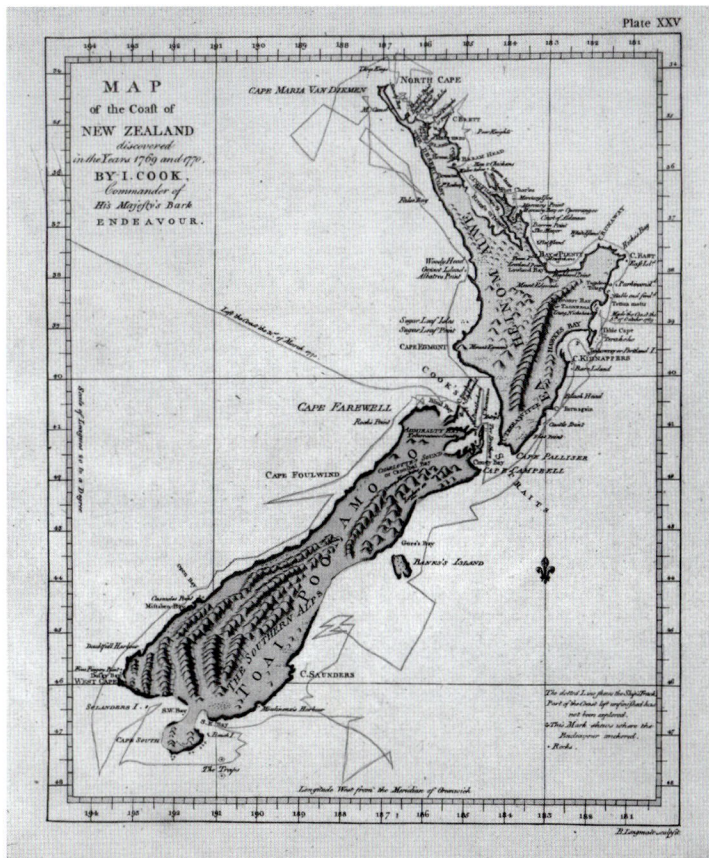

Cook's map of New Zealand.
Alexander Turnbull Library, Wellington, New Zealand, PUBL-0037-25

board named Sydney Parkinson, who sketched scenes of the new land. For fresh supplies Cook traded beads, Tahitian cloth, nails and axes with Maori. He wouldn't trade muskets. Cook wrote detailed notes about the new country. British people were interested in his information about the forests, flax, seals and whales.

Cook was responsible for making the first map of New Zealand. He made a few mistakes but, on later voyages, he corrected many of them.

Sir Joseph Banks (1743–1820). Banks' writings and images while on board the Endeavour *were significant and have provided an important record of first contact history for New Zealanders.*

Thomas Phillips, Alexander Turnbull Library, Wellington, New Zealand, A-038-017

Sydney Parkinson.

James Newton, Alexander Turnbull Library, Wellington, New Zealand, PUBL-0037-front

Cook and Ariki Tupaia

Also aboard the *Endeavour* was a Tahitian man, Ariki Tupaia. Tupaia spoke English and could communicate with Maori using his own language. In the six-month circumnavigation of the country, Tupaia helped solve many problems for the European visitors.

In October 1769, when the *Endeavour* sailed into Poverty Bay, local Maori thought the ship was a floating island. After a boat was lowered and rowed ashore, Maori ceremonially challenged the visitors. A crewman, thinking they were being attacked, shot one man dead. The next day another local was shot for snatching a sword from a sailor.

Cook, under orders not to fight, regretted the deaths. With Tupaia's help he made sure all other Maori they met knew they were friendly and only wanted to trade. There were other misunderstandings, but Cook always took time to find out what happened and acted fairly. Most Maori he met seemed to respect and admire him. Cook described Maori as, 'a strong, well-made people, active and warlike but not treacherous; a people who were both artistic and brave …'

This oil painting, created in 1905 by M.T. Clayton, depicts the Endeavour *sailing into Poverty Bay, 1769.*

Alexander Turnbull Library, Wellington, New Zealand, PAColl-3035 I/1-002134-G

Two coastal views of Poverty Bay by Sydney Parkinson. The upper view shows Young Nick's Head to the right, the lower shows cliffs and bush.

Sydney Parkinson/R.B. Godfrey, Alexander Turnbull Library, Wellington, New Zealand, PUBL-0037-14

Cook's discoveries made him a hero in his own country, in Australia and in New Zealand. New Zealand's highest mountain, the strait that separates the North and the South islands, communities, suburbs, streets, schools, parks, halls and a coin all carry his name or image.

Mt Cook.
Holger Leue

CHART
of
COOK'S STRAIT
in
NEW ZEALAND

50-cent coin

Cook found the strait between the North and South islands of New Zealand that bears his name. This map was drawn from Cook's original.
John Ryland, Alexander Turnbull Library, Wellington, New Zealand, MapColl833aj/1773/Acc. 422

9

Other Explorers and Early Contact

Captain Jean Francois Marie de Surville

In 1769, French explorer Jean de Surville saw the North Island just two months after Cook. Amazingly his ship, the *St Jean Baptiste*, passed near the *Endeavour* during a storm.

De Surville made friends with some Maori in Doubtless Bay. On Christmas Day 1769, his Catholic chaplain held the first Christian service in New Zealand. However, de Surville took action against Maori when they were seen with a ship's boat after a storm had dislodged it from the *St Jean Baptiste*. After only two weeks, de Surville sailed for South America.

Marion du Fresne

In 1772, Marion du Fresne, another French explorer, arrived at Spirit's Bay, Northland. A month later, Maori killed him and 26 of his crew for breaking tapu. To avenge the deaths, the remaining crew, led by Julien Crozet, destroyed a local village and killed almost 300 Maori.

A scuba diver alongside one of the anchors lost from the St Jean Baptiste *during a storm in 1769. The anchors were rediscovered at Doubtless Bay in 1974.*

Kelly Tarlton Collection, Alexander Turnbull Library, Wellington, New Zealand, PAColl-0412-1

Reconstruction of the death of Marion du Fresne at Spirit's Bay.

Charles Meryon, Alexander Turnbull Library, Wellington, New Zealand, G-824-3

*T*apu means sacred. Tapu is an important part of Maori life. Kumara gardens were tapu. The birth of a baby was tapu. Anyone who broke tapu was in danger of being punished.

---

*W*hen a penal colony was to be established in the South Pacific, the British Government decided to build it in New South Wales, partly because of the deaths of Europeans on Tasman's, du Fresne's and Cook's voyages, but also because the Australian Aboriginals were thought to be less organised and less war-like than Maori.

George Vancouver and William Broughton

In 1791, Englishman George Vancouver, after exploring Dusky Sound in his ship *Discovery* with his other ship, *Chatham*, commanded by William Broughton, hit a storm while sailing towards Tahiti. The *Chatham* was blown eastwards.

On the morning of 29 November, Broughton sighted a part of Chatham Island. He mapped the coastline then anchored outside Kaingaroa Harbour. Broughton and eight men went ashore and met a group of Moriori men. A misunderstanding happened during bartering and Broughton's men killed a local man. The Moriori were peaceful people, and they blamed themselves for the violence. From then on they welcomed all visitors with a grass plant instead of clubs or spears.

The burning of the Boyd

In 1809, another misunderstanding between Maori and Europeans ended in disaster. The British vessel *Boyd*, anchored in Whangaroa Harbour, was burnt by friends and family of a mistreated Maori crew member. Up to 70 Europeans were killed.

Painted in 1908 by Walter Wright, this image shows an artist's idea of what the burning of the Boyd might have looked like in 1809.
Auckland Art Gallery Toi o Tāmaki , gift of the Auckland Picture Purchase Fund, 1908

*N*ot all meetings between Maori and Europeans ended with violence. Each group saw that the ways of the other were different and the more they got to know each other the better they got along.

Some other early explorers who visited New Zealand

Jules Sebastien Cesar Dumont D'Urville (France)
Antoine-Raymond Joseph de Bruni d'Entrecasteaux (France)
Louis Isidore Duperrey (France)
Fabian Gottlieb von Bellingshausen (Russia)
Alessandro Malaspina (Spain)

Pakeha Maori

By the 1790s Sydney and Hobart were large sealing and whaling ports. Ships from Australia, crewed mostly by convicts, often sailed to New Zealand. The first Europeans to live in New Zealand escaped from these ships and joined Maori communities. They were called 'Pakeha Maori'; they married Maori women, had Maori children and followed Maori customs and beliefs. Some had Maori moko (tattoo). Pakeha Maori shared agricultural and sailing skills and acted as interpreters for traders and missionaries.

*B*arnet Burns, a tattooed Pakeha Maori who lived on the North Island's East Coast, wrote about his life among Maori. He said, 'I was made and considered a chief of a tribe of upwards of six hundred persons, consisting of men, women and children. I could purchase flax when others could not. In fact, I was well liked amongst the rest of the chiefs, as though I had been their brother …'

B. BURNS.

A NEW ZEALAND CHIEF.

Alexander Turnbull Library, Wellington, New Zealand. PUBL-0074-26

'Pakeha Maori' John Rutherford. Rutherford eventually returned to English where this watercolour of him was painted by George Scharf.
George Scharf, Alexander Turnbull Library, Wellington, New Zealand, A-090-028

*C*harlotte Badger was one of a few female Pakeha Maori. She lived in the Bay of Islands.

Sealers

In 1792, sealers from Australia came to Dusky Sound on the southwest coast of the South Island. They built the first European-style houses in New Zealand. Sealers from France and America soon followed. Dozens of sealing camps dotted the coast in Foveaux Strait and around Stewart Island. Maori, after learning to flense (to cut up and slice the fat) the seals and treat the skins, worked in many of the camps.

In the same year as their arrival, sealers took 4500 skins from Dusky Sound. In 1805, one ship, the *Favorite*, took 80,000 skins from Foveaux Strait. Between 1806 and 1810, 250,000 skins were taken from the Antipodes Islands. Seal skins were sold in China, America and England and were made into felt hats. Skins were also traded with the Chinese in Canton and Macau in exchange for tea.

Seal numbers quickly decreased. Without work, some sealers joined southern Maori tribes. They grew vegetables and traded with ships that visited Fiordland ports.

By 1830, ruthless slaughter had almost wiped out the seals on these coasts and islands and most sealers' camps had been abandoned.

Simeon Lord was one of the seal traders based in Sydney. He was quick to take advantage of New Zealand's abundant population of seals.
State Library of New South Wales, MIN 92

KILLING SEALS IN A CAVERN.

This picture of a cave in Dusky Sound shows the brutal way that seals were killed for their fur and oil.
Auckland City Libraries Tāmaki Pātaka Kōrero, John H. Clark, *Foreign field sports*, 1819

Whalers

Deep-sea whalers

In the late 1700s, to the north, south and east of New Zealand, deep-sea whalers from Britain, France and America were hunting sperm whales. The ships often came to shore for fresh supplies. In 1830, at Kororareka in the Bay of Islands, up to 30 ships could be in port at any time. Of the 1000 crewman, 300 could be on shore, mostly drinking in the taverns. As well as trading vegetables and pigs with the sailors, many Maori joined the crews.

This view of Kororareka (Russell) in the Bay of Islands, was probably drawn during the mid-1830s.
Joel Samuel Polack, Alexander Turnbull Library, Wellington, New Zealand, A-032-026

Whalers harpooning sperm whales, North Cape.
Joel Samuel Polack, Alexander Turnbull Library, Wellington, New Zealand, PUBL-0115-1-front

*W*hale stations were often built close to Maori settlements. Maori grew crops for trading and the men joined the whale hunts. They traded or were given European clothing, tools, plants and animals. They learned how to build European houses and boats. Many Maori women married shore whalers. Maori culture and values remained strong in these first mixed communities. Pakeha were there only because Maori allowed them to be.

Shore whalers

After 1820, whale stations were set up on the coast of the main islands and around Cook and Foveaux straits. From May to October, the whalers went to sea in sturdy whaleboats to hunt the right whale, which came inshore to give birth. Right whales were hunted for their oil and bones. Sperm whales were hunted for their oil, which was used in Europe for lighting.

The bones were used for women's corsets, umbrella ribs and upholstery packing.

From the 1790s, whalers made temporary visits to the north of New Zealand. A few left their ships and became shore-based traders.

A whaling station on Kapiti Island, 1844.
Walter Armiger Bowring, Alexander Turnbull Library, Wellington, New Zealand, D-018-012

The first shore whaling station

Jacky Guard, a past convict and sealer, developed the first shore whaling station in the late 1820s in the Tory Channel in the Marlborough Sounds. Guard's Australian wife, Betty, gave birth to a son, John, in 1831. John is thought to be the first 'full' Pakeha child born in the South Island.

Jacky Guard lived in the cleared area of this bay, called Kakapo Bay.
William Fox, Alexander Turnbull Library, Wellington, New Zealand, B-113-015

Like the seals, over-killing ruined the whale industry. By 1850 most whaling stations had disappeared from the coasts.

A scene showing what the artist describes as 'rimus' being felled near Wellington.
Samuel Charles Brees, Alexander Turnbull Library, Wellington, New Zealand, A-109-036

Maori were keen traders with 'pakeha'. They traded mainly potatoes and pork for nails (used as chisels, gouges and fish-hooks), and muskets and blankets. New crops such as wheat, maize, barley and oats were brought by the missionaries to New Zealand and were planted by Maori. Maori also supplied fresh food for all early visitors and settlers.

As each industry — sealing, whaling, flax and timber — grew, Maori were quick to learn new skills. Within their tribes, many became well-organised and successful merchants.

Timber

Timber was needed for ships' masts, spars and hulls. In the 1790s, five shiploads of kahikatea were taken from the banks of the Waihou River, but English ship-builders rejected the wood because it rotted in water. During the 1820s, British naval expeditions to the Coromandel Peninsula discovered kauri. James Cook had been the first to note the vast inland kauri forests during a journey up the Waihou River.

Right: Kauri with seed heads, drawn during the 1780s.
Alexander Turnbull Library, Wellington, New Zealand, PUBL-0150-006

Left: A saw mill at Kaiwharawhara, near Wellington.
Samuel Charles Brees,, Alexander Turnbull Library, Wellington, New Zealand, A-109-33

The tall, thick, flexible and branchless timber was perfect for ship-building. For 50 years Pakeha, helped by Maori communities, cut, shaped and removed almost all kauri from the Northland and Coromandel coasts.

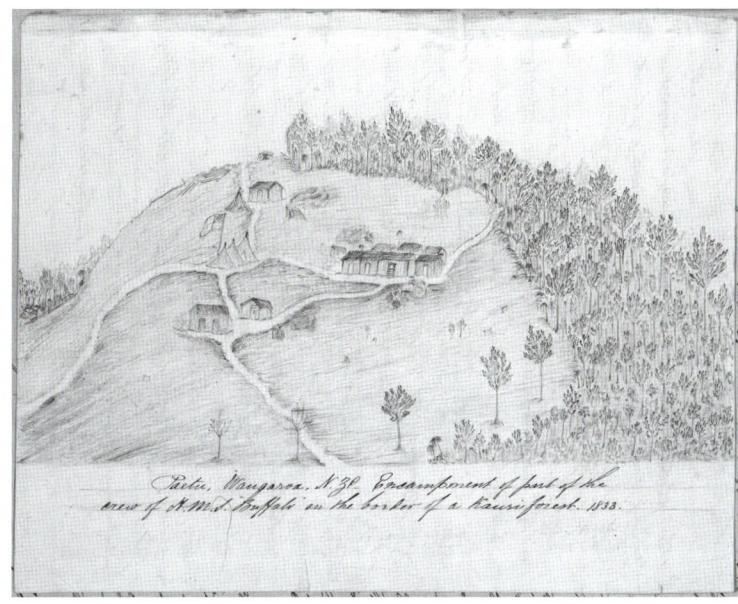

A timber camp on the border of a kauri forest, 1833.
Thomas Laslett, Alexander Turnbull Library, Wellington, New Zealand, MS-Papers-8349-1-07

Flax

The navies and fishermen around the world wanted New Zealand flax for ropes, sails, nets and sacks. Between 1825 and 1830 the flax trade boomed. Tons of flax were harvested and transported to export stations in Foveaux Strait, the Hokianga Harbour, Bay of Islands, Kawhia, Bay of Plenty and the East Coast of the North Island.

Around this time in Kawhia, Englishman John Kent married Tiria, the daughter of Waikato chief Te Wherowhero, who later became the first Maori King. An American, William Webster, married the daughter of Horeto Te Taniwha, a chief from the Coromandel Peninsula. These kinships allowed Kent and Webster to organise large numbers of local Maori to harvest huge quantities of flax and timber for export. Both Pakeha men became very wealthy.

In 1793, Norfolk Island Lieutenant-Governor Philip King had Tuki Tahua and Ngahuruhuru, from Northland, kidnapped and transported to the island to teach convicts how to prepare flax for export. It was a wasted journey. Neither man knew anything about flax preparation because it was considered women's work.

Preparing flax fibre was slow work. Maori women scraped away the green, fleshy part with the sharp edge of a mussel shell, leaving the strong, white fibre. It took about a year for one woman to prepare one ton of flax. No one was able to develop a quicker system to do this. Eventually, a better quality flax was found in the Philippines and, after 1831, the flax trade slowed.

Phormium tenax, *New Zealand flax, drawn in 1842.*
Martha King, Alexander Turnbull Library, Wellington, New Zealand, PUBL-0011-15

Old ladies plaiting flax baskets
Whanganui R.

Left: Two women plaiting flax baskets, 1861.
James Coutts Crawford, Alexander Turnbull Library, Wellington, New Zealand, E-041-059

Right: Preparing flax, Taranaki.
Alexander Turnbull Library, Wellington, New Zealand, PUBL-0169-1865-001

Muskets

Guns quickly became the trade item Maori most wanted. Maori used muskets for hunting birds and fighting other tribes. Tribes that didn't have guns knew they had to have them if they were to survive. And tribes that had them knew they needed more if they wanted to win battles. Between 1822 and 1836, many tribes were involved in musket wars.

Maori bargaining with a European, around 1845.
John Williams, Alexander Turnbull Library, Wellington, New Zealand, A-079-017

Sydney-based flax merchants and whalers were the primary traders of muskets. In 1814, one musket was worth 150 baskets of potatoes or eight pigs. By 1820, one musket was worth 200 baskets of potatoes or 15 pigs.

As the surviving tribes became armed, they were better able to defend themselves. The fighting ended around 1839. More than 20,000 Maori were killed during the tribal musket wars.

Hongi Hika

In 1820, famous Ngapuhi chief Hongi Hika visited England with the missionary Thomas Kendall. There he helped scholars put together a book on the Maori language. He was very popular and he was given many gifts. King George IV gave him a full suit of armour. Hongi Hika kept the armour but sold his other gifts and bought 500 muskets.

When Hongi Hika wore his armour into battle, his enemies thought he was unconquerable. When he wasn't at war, Hongi Hika lived at Waimate. Missionary Samuel Marsden described him as 'a very fine character … mild in his manners and very polite.' Hongi Hika died in 1828 from an infected bullet wound.

Hongi Hika.
Arnold Frederick Goodwin, Alexander Turnbull Library, Wellington, New Zealand, A-236-006

Religion

Early Maori beliefs

Maori have always had their own gods and believed the mind, body and spirit were connected and affected by daily life. But, unlike Christians, they didn't believe all people — chiefs, commoners, women, children — were equal in the eyes of the gods. Maori gods included Rangi-nui, the Sky Father, and Papatuanuku, the Earth Mother. From Rangi and Papa came their children, Tane-mahuta, God of the Forests; Tumatauenga, God of War; Rongo-ma-tane, God of Peace; Tangaroa, God of the Sea; Tawhiri-matea, God of the Winds; and Ruaimoko, God of Earthquakes and Volcanic Power.

Sunrise

Tama-nui-te-ra (the Sun) is the sun god. He has two wives who represent the seasons, and he divides his time between Hine-takurua, the autumn and winter maiden, and Hine-raumati, the spring and summer maiden. In this way, changes in natural world, such as the seasons, were seen to be integrated with human ancestry. Maori experienced little separation between the human and natural worlds. Tanerore is the son of Tama-nui-te ra, and he can be seen dancing on the horizon in shimmering waves of heat.

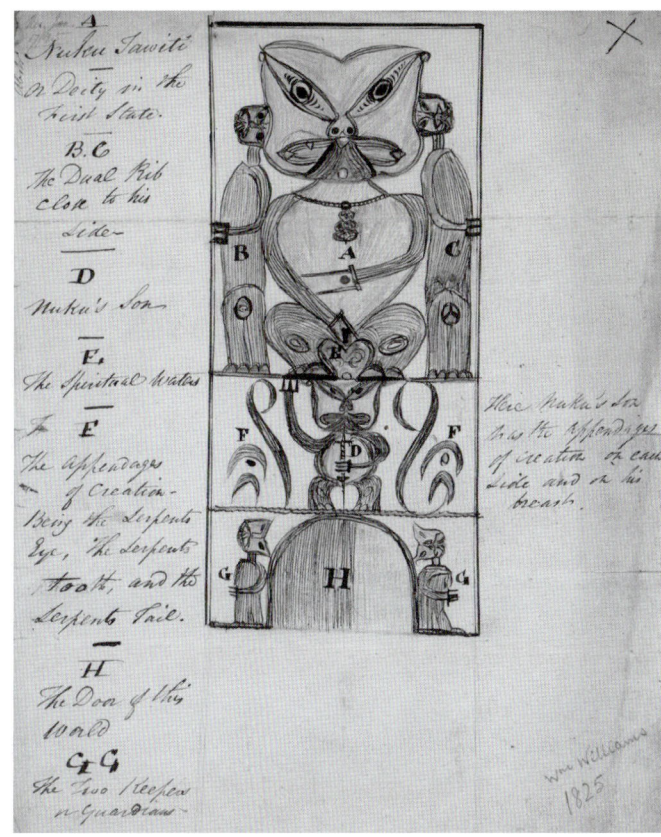

*A drawing by missionary Thomas Kendall depicting his interpretation of Maori symbology. His explanation reads, '**A** Nuku Tawiti, a Deity in the first state **B C** the dual rib close to his sides **D** Nuku's son **E** the spiritual waters **F** the appendages of creation being the serpent's eye, the serpent's tooth and the serpent's tail **H** the door of this world **G G** the two keepers or guardians.*

Thomas Kendall, Alexander Turnbull Library, Wellington, New Zealand, A-114-045

The bush

The deep bush, a source of birds, was also the haunt of fairy folk and ogres. In the North Island ogres were known as maero and were especially feared. They were said to have retreated to the forests of Taranaki and Whanganui when people arrived from Hawaiiki. In the South Island rainforests the ogres were known as maeroero, and were said to pounce on unwary travellers.

Missionaries

The first missionaries came to New Zealand to change Maori from heathens to Christians. The missionaries — William Hall, a carpenter, John King, a shoemaker and Thomas Kendall, a teacher — were led by Samuel Marsden, a wealthy landowner, Anglican chaplain and magistrate in New South Wales.

Marsden arrived in the Bay of Islands and preached his first sermon to a mostly Maori congregation on Christmas Day, 1814. In January 1815, he preached to groups in Waimate and Omapere, before returning to Australia. Hall, King and Kendall stayed in New Zealand to trade with Maori and to instruct them in horticulture, agriculture and then to make them Christians.

Landing of Samuel Marsden at the Bay of Islands, 19 December 1814.
Alexander Turnbull Library, Wellington, New Zealand, PUBL-0158-76

*S*amuel Marsden and his missionaries were members of the Church of England's Church Missionary Society (CMS). The CMS members hoped that by teaching Maori to farm, they would also become interested in learning about Christianity.

Reverend Samuel Marsden.
Richard Read, Alexander Turnbull Library, Wellington, New Zealand, A-039-038

Samuel Marsden giving the first Christian Church service in New Zealand, 24 December 1814.
Jack Morgan, Alexander Turnbull Library, Wellington, New Zealand, B-077-002

Church Missionary Society settlement at 'Kiddeekiddee' (Kerikeri).
Church Missionary quarterly papers, Alexander Turnbull Library, Wellington, New Zealand, PUBL-0031-30

Church Missionary Society settlement at Rangihoua, 1832.
Church Missionary quarterly papers, Alexander Turnbull Library, Wellington, New Zealand, PUBL-0031-1832-66

Mission stations

Samuel Marsden chose Rangihoua for the first mission station. The land belonged to his friend and protector, Ruatara, who died soon after the missionaries arrived. Hongi Hika became the missionaries' new protector and another station was built at Kerikeri.

Kendall, Hall and King were unsuccessful missionaries. They didn't work well together; they traded muskets and alcohol and they didn't speak Maori. Kendall became friendly with Hongi Hika. He tried to learn and write the Maori language, but in 1822 he was dismissed by Marsden for drunkenness and neglecting his missionary duties.

A mission station included a chapel, a schoolhouse, and buildings for the missionaries, their families and visitors.

Reverend Thomas Kendall with Ngapuhi chiefs Waikato (left) and Hongi Hika.
James Barry, Alexander Turnbull Library, vWellington, New Zealand, G-618

Marsden had met Hongi Hika when he visited Sydney. In 1809, Marsden helped Ruatara, a Maori sailor, get back to Sydney after he'd been stranded in London. Ruatara and Hongi Hika allowed missions to be built at Rangihoua and Kerikeri because the stations brought lots of trading for their people.

This view of Paihia, looking north along the beachline, includes the houses and gardens of the Church Missionary Society station, which was home to the Reverend Henry Williams and his family.

Louise Auguste de Sainson, Alexander Turnbull Library, Wellington, New Zealand, B-052-019

There were gardens and orchards but the missionaries had to trade with local Maori for other supplies.

Most Maori had little respect for the missionaries. They didn't want to know about Christianity. They thought the missionaries were poor traders and didn't have many useful skills. By 1822, eight years after their arrival, the missionaries still hadn't converted any Maori to Christianity. Hongi Hika said, 'Christianity is unsuitable for a nation of warriors and fit only for a nation of slaves.'

Other missionaries

The Reverend John Butler was the first resident clergyman in New Zealand. He came to the Bay of Islands in 1819. With his helpers, James and Charlotte Kemp, he set up the mission station at Kerikeri. Butler was dismissed for drunkenness and, in 1823, Samuel Marsden appointed Reverend Henry Williams as the new Anglican missionary superintendent.

Waimate North mission station, 1845.

Cyprian Bridge, Alexander Turnbull Library, Wellington, New Zealand, PUBL-0144-1-330

The HMS Herald.

Williams built a mission station at Paihia. He stopped
missionaries trading muskets and he made sure they all,
including himself and his brother, learned the Maori language.
When Maori heard about Christianity in their own language,
they became more interested.

Williams and Marsden opened mission stations at Kaitaia,
Waimate, Maraetai, Kauaeranga, Puriri, Matamata,
Mangapopouri, Rotorua, Otaka and Waikanae. By 1842,
there were over 3000 Christian Maori in the North Island.

James and Charlotte Kemp's house at Kerikeri is New
Zealand's oldest surviving European residence. Kemp's Stone
Store, completed in 1836, is the oldest commercial building.

Henry Williams, an ex-Royal Navy officer, had studied
medicine and had carpentry and boat-building skills. He built
a trading ship called the Herald, and used his ship to visit
and trade with Maori in other parts of New Zealand. He
often helped warring tribes make peace. His brother William
compiled the first Maori dictionary.

Henry Williams.

Changing beliefs

Maori admired the Williams' and Kemps' honourable way of living. They were keen to learn to read and write their own language. Missionaries were often peacemakers in tribal wars. When Maori became ill with European diseases such as influenza and measles, missionaries' medicines cured many people.

Maori wanted farming, carpentry and boat-building skills. Slowly, particularly in the North where most missionaries were, Maori changed their ideas about Christianity and, to some extent, combined the new beliefs with their own beliefs.

Christianity was also spread by slaves captured by Ngapuhi during the musket wars. Many of the slaves, freed by missionaries, went home and shared their beliefs with their new tribes. In 1836, Piripi Taumata-a-kura, a freed slave from Ngati Porou (East Coast) took Christianity to his people.

Missionary and printer William Colenso brought a printing press to the Paihia mission in 1834. Demand was high for copies of William Williams' Maori translation of the Bible. New beliefs also meant that some Maori traditions were no longer practiced, such as cannibalism or having more than one wife.

NIGHT SCENE IN NEW ZEALAND.

A group of Maori listening to a missionary preacher, reportedly James Kemp, 1837.
William Richard Wade, Alexander Turnbull Library, Wellington, New Zealand, PUBL-0031-37

The Wesleyan Church

In 1822, Wesleyan missionaries William White, Nathaniel Turner and John Hobbs were helped by the Anglican missionaries to build a Methodist mission at Whangaroa. Nathaniel Turner was a farmer. William White was more of a trader than a missionary and John Hobbs, a carpenter, shifted to the Tongan mission in 1831.

The Wesleyans wanted to 'propose the Gospel in its simplest and most explicit truths'. They did not want to own land or trade with Maori. Early attempts to turn local Maori into Christians were not successful and, in 1827, the Whangaroa station was attacked and destroyed by a Maori war party. The Whangaroa station wasn't rebuilt. A new station was established at Mangunga on the shores of the Hokianga Harbour.

During the 1830s, the Wesleyans worked in areas the Anglicans had not. They built new stations in Tangiteroria, beside the Wairoa River, Raglan and Kawhia. Tainui Maori in the Waikato became the largest group of Wesleyan followers.

Reverend Nathaniel Turner.
John Cochran, Alexander Turnbull Library, Wellington, New Zealand, A-042-019

Below: An early Methodist station, Whangaroa Harbour.
Alexander Turnbull Library, Wellington, New Zealand, B-121-024

WESLEYAN MISSION-PREMISES AT KAWHIA, NEW ZEALAND.

Wesleyan mission at Kawhia.
Alexander Turnbull Library, Wellington, New Zealand, PUBL-0139-105

The Catholic Church

The Anglican and Wesleyan missionaries were not friendly to the Catholic missionaries when they arrived on the shores of the Hokianga Harbour in 1838. Nathaniel Turner sent local Maori across the harbour to attack the first Catholic station at Totara Point but it was easily protected by Te Rarawa Maori. Bishop Jean-Baptiste Pompallier was the Catholic leader. He was helped by priests and some Irish-Catholic settlers.

The Catholic missionaries didn't have families so they covered more of the country quicker than the Anglicans or Wesleyans. By 1841, Pompallier had established twelve stations throughout the country.

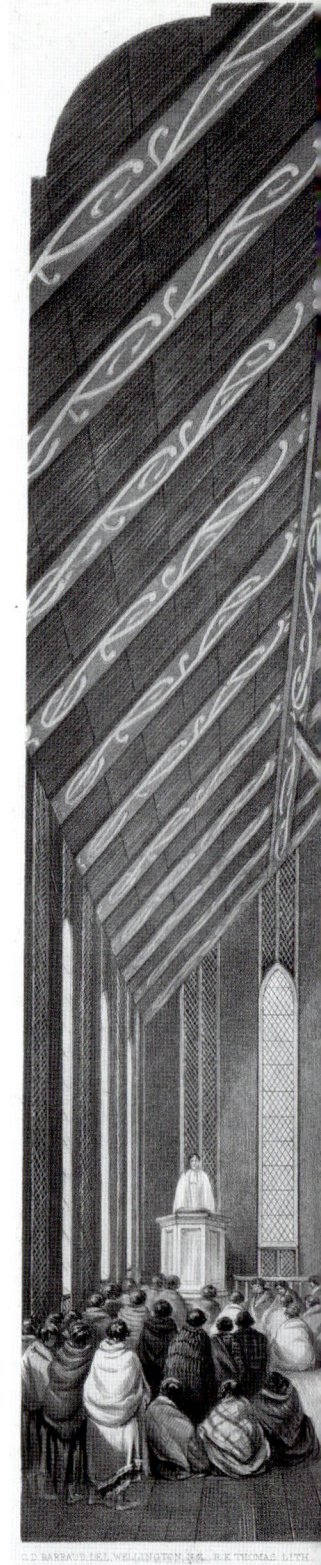

Interior of Rangiatea Church at Otaki, an Anglican church.
Charles Decimus Barraud, Alexander Turnbull Library, Wellington, New Zealand, B-080-021

The English Anglicans and Wesleyans were not friendly with the French Catholics because England and France had recently been at war.

The first Catholic mission was built on Thomas Poynton's land. He was one of about 50 Catholics who lived in the Hokianga during the 1830s.

Pompallier was 36 years old when he arrived in New Zealand. Maori were impressed with his flowing purple robes, sash and tasseled hat. With Poynton's help, he was preaching in Maori after about three months.

In 1839, the mission was moved from Hokianga to Russell. The mission house is still standing today.

Bishop Jean-Baptiste Francois Pompallier.
J. Meunier, Alexander Turnbull Library, Wellington, New Zealand, NON-ATL-0061

Roman catholic Chapel — *Rangawahia* — *were the Skirmish took place Priest's House & School*

Above: The Roman Catholic chapel at Rangiaohia.
Charles Eastwood, Alexander Turnbull Library, Wellington, New Zealand, A-128-023

Left: A Catholic chapel in Wellington.
Samuel Charles Brees, Alexander Turnbull Library, Wellington, New Zealand, E-070-003

New religions

After hearing all the missionaries in the Hokianga area talk about religion, Papahurihia, a Ngapuhi tohunga, developed his own religion. He used ideas from Maori, Christian and Jewish beliefs. He and his followers believed they were like the Israelites of the Old Testament- they were the Chosen of God and 'Jews' not Christian.

Papahurihia was a clever ventriloquist. During sermons, he often created 'spirit voices and noises' that impressed his followers. Papahurihia didn't like the Anglican missionaries. He called them murderers and witchcraft performers. When he changed his name to Te Atua Wera — the fiery god — his religion became known as Papahurihia.

Today, some people in the southern Hokianga, have Papahurihia beliefs.

Law and Order

New Zealand was a 'lawless land'. Traders exporting goods to Australia, the missionaries and other British people living in New Zealand wanted order and protection. Northern Maori had also written to the King of England in 1831 asking for protection against a visiting armed French ship. So, in 1832, the Governor of New South Wales sent James Busby to New Zealand as the first British Resident. Busby was like a diplomat. He represented British law and order but he wasn't able to enforce it. Maori called Busby, 'Man o' War without guns'.

In 1839, former British convict Edward Gibbon Wakefield made it known that he wanted to settle hundreds of immigrants in New Zealand. He also wanted to form a government there. The British government sent William Hobson, a naval captain, to New Zealand with instructions to persuade Maori chiefs to recognise Queen Victoria's authority so that New Zealand could be governed by Britain.

James Hector Busby.
James Ingram McDonald, Alexander Turnbull Library, Wellington, New Zealand, A-044-008

Hobson arrived in the Bay of Islands on 29 January 1840. He was to be the Lieutenant-Governor of New Zealand under the authority of the Governor of New South Wales. A few days later he convinced many Maori chiefs to sign the Treaty of Waitangi. This was probably the most important event in New Zealand's history.

Busby had no soldiers or policemen to help him keep law and order. In 1834, he gathered northern Maori chiefs together to choose a flag to fly on New Zealand ships. They chose a red St George's Cross on a white background with four eight-point stars. Many thousands of Europeans had visited New Zealand but only 2000 had stayed.

Sealers', whalers', sailors' and missionaries' tales of New Zealand's good climate, excellent farmland and friendly Maori were starting to attract more settlers.

Edward Gibbon Wakefield offered land in New Zealand — which he did not own — for sale in London.

Edward Gibbon Wakefield.
Abraham Wivell/B. Holt, Alexander Turnbull Library, Wellington, New Zealand, A-042-023

Captain William Hobson, first Governor of New Zealand.
James Ingram McDonald, Alexander Turnbull Library, Wellington, New Zealand, G-826-1

'The government gave the New Zealanders a flag or rather one under which the vessels sail …'
Edward Markham, Alexander Turnbull Library, Wellington, New Zealand, MS-1550-120

The Treaty of Waitangi

When Britain finally decided to annex New Zealand, it took possession of the country not on the grounds of discovery or by force of arms, but by signing a treaty with the Māori people. Under the Treaty of Waitangi of 1840, Māori passed sovereignty to Britain in return for guarantees about their land and other possessions. No pictures were made at the time the Treaty was signed.

A sheet from The Treaty of Waitangi signed at Waitangi. There are nine sheets of signatures that make up the Treaty, many obtained when the document was taken around New Zealand.
Archives New Zealand/Te Rua Mahara o te Kawanatanga, Wellington Office, Archives reference: IA 9/9

THE SIGNING OF THE TREATY OF WAITANGI FEBRUARY 6, 1840.

The day that New Zealand became a part of the British Empire. The painting displays the historical group assembled at the residence of Mr. James Busby, British Resident, at Waitangi, Bay of Islands, to meet Captain William Hobson, R.N., first Governor of New Zealand. The Rev. Henry Williams acted as interpreter, explaining the terms of the Treaty to the Maori chiefs. Principals in the impressive and historical scene included Mr. Williams, Captain Joseph Nias, R.N., Captain Hobson and Mr. Busby. The Maori chief in the act of signing the Treaty is Tamati Waka Nene.

This reconstruction of the signing of the Treaty of Waitangi, painted by Marcus King in 1939, gives a reasonably accurate depiction of who was there.
Marcus King, Alexander Turnbull Library, Wellington, New Zealand, 82-419-01

The word 'pakeha' was used in the Treaty of Waitangi to mean non-Maori subjects of the Queen. However, it had been in use as early as 1814, when Missionary William Hall wrote that he'd been called 'rungateeda pakehaa' (rangitira pakeha — European gentleman).

The Maori population

Maori had no immunity to the diseases Europeans brought to New Zealand. Many died from influenza, measles and whooping cough. Epidemics happened mainly in the places that Europeans visited and settled, such as the Bay of Islands, Foveaux Strait and the Coromandel Peninsula. The diseases did not spread to places were Europeans rarely went such as the Waikato, King Country, Urewera, inland Hawkes Bay and Wairarapa.

In 1769, the estimated Maori population was 100,000 people. By 1839, the musket wars and epidemics had lowered this number to around 70,000.

New Zealand Aotearoa

Before 1840 the main areas of contact between Maori and Europeans were at opposite ends of the country. Sealers and whalers frequented the shores of Foveaux Strait, in the South Island. They also called in to the Bay of Islands in Northland for rest, recreation and supplies. There, Kororareka (now Russell) developed as New Zealand's first rough and ready European town.

Although Europeans brought many changes to New Zealand — clothes, guns, blankets, steel tools, potatoes, turnips, grains, new beliefs and written Maori and English — Maori outnumbered Europeans by ten to one. More changes were to happen, but in 1840, the year the Treaty was signed, New Zealand was still a Maori world.

A view of Kororareka (Russell), painted during the mid-1830s.
Augustus Earle, Alexander Turnbull Library, Wellington, New Zealand, PUBL-0015-06

Index

NOTE: numbers in bold indicate imagery